CONTENTS

3 5444 00100063 6

D0921965

Introduction. 4

A few facts 5

A little history 6

Music and literature 12

Food and drink 17

Customs, values and traditions 24

Sport 51

Places worth seeing 55

Further information.. 60

INTRODUCTION

Welcome to *Meet the English*, an original and sometimes humorous look at what makes England England, and the English, oh so English. I have included addresses to relevant websites for topics you might like to explore in greater depth. It may be that between writing and publication some of the websites have disappeared, for which I apologise; such is the transient nature of the World Wide Web.

Visitors from overseas please note that on each page there is a section entitled 'Metaphorically Speaking.' The English love using metaphors and, if English is not your native language, this can cause confusion. 'Metaphorically Speaking' will introduce you to just a few of the many metaphors you might hear during your stay. Try using them and impress your hosts with your excellent command of their language.

I hope you enjoy reading this book, that it makes you laugh, and that it leaves you feeling at least slightly more knowledgeable than before you started it. If you're a visitor to this green and pleasant land you are very welcome, and please remember to spend lots of money.

A FEW FACTS

Population
As of August 2007 approximately 51 million with an average age of 39.5 and rising.

Climate
Variable, depending on the time of year and the part of the country you visit.

Currency
Coins (pence; pounds): 1p, 2p, 5p, 10p, 20p; £1, £2
Notes (pounds): £5, £10, £20, £50

Currency conversion
Even though the English have had decimalization for many years you may still hear people referring to units from pre-decimalization:
A shilling = 5p
Ten bob = 50p
A quid = One pound
A guinea = £1.05 (still used in the One thousand and Two thousand guineas horse races)

Coastline
England has approximately 5581 miles of it, and there is no point in England that is more than 75 miles from the coast, so always bring a bucket and spade.

Size
Does size really matter? Because, if it does, small is best. American, Australian and Japanese visitors especially might be interested in the following: In geographic size England is 75 times smaller than the USA, 58 times smaller than Australia and 2.8 times smaller than Japan.

A RIGHT ROYAL BATTLE

The Battle of Hastings was fought on October 14th 1066 between Harold II of England and Duke William of Normandy. During the battle Harold was shot in the eye and killed. With the English army defeated, William, commonly referred to as William the Conqueror, was crowned king on Christmas Day that same year. Most importantly for many English people, this was the very last time a foreign army successfully invaded Merry Old England. www.battle1066.com

Metaphorically Speaking   *Metaphor:*   *Getting Joe to clean his room is a battle of wills*
                                              Meaning: *Getting Joe to clean his room is very difficult*

DRAGONS, SAINTS AND FLAGS

St George – dragon slayer and patron saint of England – provided the banner from which the English flag is derived. First introduced by King Richard I, the flag is a red cross on a white background, and is flown across the land on 23rd April when England celebrates St George's day. www.britannia.com

Metaphorically Speaking   *Metaphor: Our landlady is a real dragon*
                                     Meaning: Our landlady is really fierce and unfriendly

HADRIAN'S WALL

Even as long ago as AD 122 the Scots were causing problems for the English, and so the Roman emperor, Hadrian, had the wonderful idea of building a wall to keep them out. Stretching the 73.5 miles (117 kilometres) from the Solway Firth in the west to the River Tyne in the east, it worked for quite some time, but, in the end, even a wall wasn't enough.
www.hadrians-wall.org

Metaphorically Speaking Metaphor: _Their questions were met by a wall of silence_
Meaning: _No one would answer their questions_

ROYALTY

The first recorded King of England was Egbert of Wessex who ruled between 827 and 839 AD. Since then England's royal heritage, along with the royal family itself, has possibly become one of the biggest tourist attractions in the world. The Queen is more recognizable than the Pope; but then, having your face on all the money probably helps.
www.royal.gov.uk

Metaphorically Speaking

Metaphor:	*It is the jewel in the crown of the collection*
Meaning:	*It is the very best piece in the collection*

BONFIRE NIGHT

On the 5th of November 1605 Guy Fawkes, a Roman Catholic conspirator, tried to blow up King James I at the state opening of Parliament in what became known as the Gunpowder Plot. He failed, and now every year the English celebrate when they:

> *Remember remember the 5th of November*
> *Gunpowder treason and plot*
> *We see no reason*
> *Why gunpowder treason*
> *Should ever be forgot!*

The celebrations usually take the form of firework displays, both public and private (where families set off fireworks in their own gardens), but in a few places, notably Lewes in Sussex, there are processions through the town, culminating in an effigy of the Pope being burned on a bonfire.
www.bonfirenight.net

Metaphorically Speaking

Metaphor: There will be fireworks when his wife finds out how much he spent in the pub

Meaning: His wife will be angry when she finds out how much he spent in the pub

MANCHESTER'S BABY

Yes, we all know about Microsoft, Apple, IBM and Dell, but the first machine that can be considered a computer, Babbage's Difference Engine, was built by Charles Babbage, a professor at Cambridge University, in 1834. England's first electronic computer was built by Manchester University. Known as 'the Baby' it ran its first successful programme on June 21st 1948.
www.computer50.org

Metaphorically Speaking

Metaphor:
Computers seldom work like clockwork

Meaning:
Computers seldom work without any problems

MORRIS DANCING

No this is not about a man called Morris who likes to dance. Neither is it about the rather cute car once favoured by vicars and Miss Marple-like little old ladies. This is about the tradition of Morris Dancing, which, in England, dates back to around the 15th century, and is today a uniquely traditional English folk dance. Mind you, what with the strange costumes and weird movements, it can sometimes look pretty silly. www.morrisdancing.org

Metaphorically Speaking

Metaphor:	*The thieves led the police a merry dance before they were caught*
Meaning:	*The thieves caused the police a lot of problems before they were caught*

SEX WITH A BANG

Appealing to the rebel lurking in even the most conservative and law-abiding English man and woman, the Sex Pistols were formed in London in 1975. Possibly the best-known punk rock band ever, even though they only made one album: *Never Mind the Bollocks, Here's the Sex Pistols*, released on 29th October 1977. www.sexpistolsofficial.com

Metaphorically Speaking

Metaphor: *George was forced to face the music when his parents found out what he had done*
Meaning: *George was criticised and punished by his parents when they found out what he had done*

GLASTONBURY FESTIVAL

The first festival was held on 19th September 1970 with tickets costing £1 each. (Incidentally, this was the day after Jimmy Hendrix died.) It is held in the open and it nearly always rains heavily, turning the ground to mud. But, despite this, the Glastonbury Festival has grown from an initial attendance of 1500 into the largest music and performing arts festival in the world!

Metaphorically Speaking

Metaphor:
Hearing that Oxford beat Cambridge in the boat race was music to my ears

Meaning:
I was very pleased to hear that Oxford beat Cambridge

LITERATURE

Nobody knows exactly how many books have been published in English around the world. England itself has given birth to many literary greats. William Shakespeare, Charles Dickens, Thomas Hardy, Somerset Maugham, and Jane Austin are just a few of the great names from English literature many will recognise immediately. The first book ever printed in the English language, however, was *Recuyell of the Histories of Troy*, a translation by William Caxton from the original French of Raol Lefèvre. www.online-literature.com

Metaphorically Speaking

Metaphor: *He's very easy to read*
Meaning: *It's easy to tell what he is thinking*

POETRY

As well as great writers, England is also a land of great poets. The earliest known English poem dates from around the middle of the 7th century, and is believed to be by an Anglo Saxon herdsman called Caedmon who worked for Whitby Abbey. Some poets have even become tourist attractions, like William Wordsworth, who has his very own dedicated museum at Grasmere in the Lake District, where he lived at Dove Cottage from December 1799 to May 1808. There are far too many to list, but some of the better-known English poets also include William Blake, Elizabeth Barrett Browning, Robert Browning, Lord Byron, Robert Graves, John Keats, Shelley, and Alfred Lord Tennyson.

Metaphorically Speaking *Metaphor:* *There is a poetic justice in what just happened*
Meaning: *What just happened is a fair punishment for what they did*

SUNDAY ROAST AND PUDDING

Whoever tells you English food is boring has never had a traditional English Sunday roast. Roast beef, roast potatoes, Yorkshire pudding (not sweet), vegetables and gravy: simply the best!

Once the roast beef has been eaten and the gravy mopped up, it's time for pudding. The English love their puddings and no dinner is complete without one. Traditional favourites include sticky toffee pudding, sherry trifle, jam roly-poly, and, at Christmas time, plum pudding (which, incidentally, does not contain plums). But remember, if you don't eat your greens, you won't get any pudding.

Metaphorically Speaking

Metaphor: After many years of marriage she felt the need to spice up their relationship
Meaning: After many years of marriage she felt the need to add some excitement to their relationship

FISH, CHIPS AND CURRY

You can't be English, or visit England, and not eat (and hopefully love) the national dish. Fish and chips rule, OK! So, if you want to make a friend, offer them a chip. The first chips were actually fried in Oldham, Lancashire, in around 1860, marking the beginning of the fast food revolution. The biggest fish and chip shop in the world can also be found in England. Harry Ramsden's, in Guiseley in the county of West Yorkshire, has seats for over 250 diners, and comes complete with oak panelling, wall-to-wall carpets, crystal chandeliers, and stained glass windows!

Curry, however, first introduced to England by nineteenth century soldiers and administrators who had spent time in India, is fast catching up with fish and chips as the country's favourite dish. In the north of England head for the 'curry mile' in Rusholme, Manchester. In the south, Brick Lane in London is the place to be.
www.federationoffishfriers.co.uk, www.rusholmecurry.co.uk, www.visitbricklane.com

Metaphorically Speaking   *Metaphor: There is something very fishy about this*
                             Meaning: There is something very suspicious about this

THE FULL ENGLISH

Breakfast like a king, lunch like a prince, and dine like a pauper, or so the saying goes. Sausage, bacon and eggs, a whole empire was built on the full English breakfast. In these days of healthy eating, however, the English are more likely to have bran for breakfast than bacon, and look what's happened to the Empire!

Of course, toast is also an important part of breakfast in England, but instead of marmalade (a Scottish invention) try some Marmite instead. This thick, dark, savoury spread is made from concentrated yeast sludge, a by-product created during the beer brewing process. You'll either love it or you'll hate it, but Marmite has been around since 1902 so must have more lovers than haters. Go on, dip yourself in the stuff, and get a Marmite lover to lick it off. www.marmite.co.uk

Metaphorically Speaking

Metaphor: *He was left with egg on his face when they found out he had made such a big mistake*

Meaning: *He was very embarrassed when they found out he had made such a big mistake*

THE SANDWICH

OK, so the Americans make bigger ones, but the sandwich was invented in England when the Earl of Sandwich, an inveterate gambler, ordered his servants to bring him "A steak placed between two pieces of bread," so he could eat without leaving the gaming tables.

http://www.sandwichproject.co.uk/about/index.php

Metaphorically Speaking

Metaphor:
He was so hungry he wolfed down his sandwich in seconds

Meaning:
He was so hungry he ate his sandwich very quickly

A BITTER DRINK

Lager may be the drink of choice of the young, but English ale has been the drink of gentlemen for 2000 years. In medieval England ale was commonly drunk at breakfast, so when you order your English breakfast insist on a glass of ale for extra authenticity. The beer pump also originates from England, invented by Yorkshireman Joseph Bramah of Stainborough in 1797. www.camra.org.uk

Metaphorically Speaking　　Metaphor:　*She is very bitter about the divorce*
　　　　　　　　　　　　　　Meaning:　*She is very angry and upset about the divorce*

TIME FOR WINE

If ale is not to your liking there is always wine. The Romans first brought wine to England's shores, and by the time of the Domesday Survey in the late 11th century, there were 46 recorded vineyards in southern England. Today, there are around 400, producing a total of 2 million bottles a year! So yes, the English do make wine, and yes, it is very good; some might even say excellent.   www.english-wine.com, www.englishwineproducers.com

Metaphorically Speaking   Metaphor: *John has been on the wagon for almost five years*
Meaning: *John hasn't been drinking alcohol for almost five years*

WHOSE ROUND?

No matter what your tipple, there can surely be no better place to enjoy it than an English pub.

The most common name for a pub in England is 'The Red Lion' of which there were 603 at the last count. If you want something unique, though, (and a good selection of ales) visit the 17th century coaching Inn 'The Lower Red Lion' Fishpool Street, St Albans, Hertfordshire, the only pub of that particular name in the world.

Understanding the rules of etiquette is also an important part of visiting an English pub. Perhaps the most important rule of all is that of 'getting your round in.' This is the custom of buying a drink for everyone in your own group (yourself included). In the best of English traditions it is completely fair as everyone else will also take their turn. Once you've got the drinks in, why not also have a go at another pub favourite, darts, a game that dates from the Middle Ages.

Whatever pub you decide to down a pint or two in, hopefully both the beer and the welcome are equally warm and you score a bullseye at the dartboard.

Metaphorically Speaking

Metaphor: It's your shout
Meaning: It's your turn to get and pay for the drinks

www.lowerredlion.co.uk

HATING THE FRENCH

We eat their food, drink their wine, drive their cars, buy up as much of their land and property as we can, and do our best to murder their language at every opportunity. Do the English really hate the French? Mais c'est la vie mon ami, n'est pas?

Metaphorically Speaking   *Metaphor:*   *They make my blood boil*
                                           Meaning: *They make me very angry*

JOIN THE QUEUE

We queue we do and we like it too, and all I can say is, so should you. Queuing is correct and proper and brings order and civility to waiting. Capital punishment was formally abolished in England on 27th January 1999, but many English people would still happily hang a queue-jumper.

Metaphorically Speaking

Metaphor: I hate people who jump the queue

Meaning: I hate people who push into a queue and don't wait patiently for their turn

25

METRIC MADNESS

The English still like to measure in feet and inches, weigh in pounds and ounces, fill their cars by the gallon, drink beer by the pint, race horses by the furlong, run by the yard, and drive by the mile. The rest of the world should learn to live with it.
www.metric-conversion-tables.com

Metaphorically Speaking

Metaphor: No matter how hard they tried to get the price down the salesman would not give an inch
Meaning: No matter how hard they tried to get the price down the salesman would not agree to a reduction

HOME AND GARDEN

It can be cold and draughty but, nevertheless, an Englishman's home is his castle. In contrast to any chill however, the welcome you receive, if invited to visit, will always be warm.

Almost every English home has its own garden, even if it is sometimes no bigger than a postage stamp. The English love their gardens, from the humble cottage variety to the huge country estates. Today, visiting garden centres is one of the most popular leisure activities in the country. These days you don't often see anyone sipping afternoon tea or playing croquet in one, but there is still nothing more English than an English garden.

www.english-country-garden.com

| ***Metaphorically Speaking*** | *Metaphor:* | *They have a lovely garden because his wife has green fingers* |
| | *Meaning:* | *They have a lovely garden because his wife is a good gardener* |

HEROES AND LEGENDS

The English love heroes, and they have quite a few, both real and imagined. Here are three you may have heard of:

Robin Hood, protecting the good people of Sherwood from the wicked tax-man. The true identity of Robin has always been open to question. Some stories have him as a commoner, others as the dispossessed Earl of Huntingdon. This popular hero robbed the rich to feed the poor, or so the legend goes. Whether 'tis true or not, the English have hated paying their taxes ever since.
www.boldoutlaw.com

Metaphorically Speaking

Metaphor:
The prices on this menu are daylight robbery

Meaning:
The prices on this menu are far too expensive

James Bond, keeping the country safe from dangerous foreign powers. Yes, he's been portrayed by a Scotsman and an Irishman, and someone even once dared suggest an American for the job, but there is still no-one more English than 007.
www.mi6.co.uk

Last but not least, Sir Richard Branson, the Virgin billionaire. Helping to keep the economy going, providing employment, increasing GDP, and reducing the national debt.
www.virgin.com

29

COUNTRYSIDE PURSUITS

The countryside is as important to the English as water is to fish. Those that live in the countryside do everything they can to protect it, while the motorways are choked with cars every weekend and Bank Holiday as people flee the hustle and bustle of the city and try to fill up the countryside. This means that, outside of the working week, you are more likely to find peace and quiet in the suburbs of a city than the heart of the countryside.

Countryside activities are gaining in popularity year-on-year. Fishing has long been a favourite, along with rambling, mountain biking, climbing, hang-gliding, pot-holing, and anything else that can be done in wellies and a waterproof.

Metaphorically Speaking   Metaphor: *She is always fishing for compliments*
                                        Meaning: *She is always trying to get people to say nice things about her*

PRIVATE PROPERTY

If visiting from abroad you should know that almost all land in England is privately owned, and right of access is limited to marked public footpaths. While some land owners would like nothing better than to shoot trespassers, the more liberal majority are happy just to politely ask you to leave. Thankfully, there are ten National Parks in England, encompassing some of the most beautiful countryside in the country, where visitors are free to wander in peace providing they follow the countryside code. http://www.naturalengland.org.uk

Metaphorically Speaking   *Metaphor:*   *Jack landed a job straight after leaving university*
                               Meaning: *Jack got a job immediately after leaving university*

A CLASS FOR EVERYONE

The English class system is alive and kicking, but less noticeable than it once was. Aristocrats don't always sound like they have a plum in their mouths these days, and the working class stopped wearing cloth caps and clogs a long time ago. Nowadays, the aristocracy wear the cloth caps, usually while out huntin', shootin', and fishin'. It's all very confusing to know one's place any more.

Metaphorically Speaking   Metaphor: *He's very nice but his wife is really stuck-up*
                                  Meaning: *He's very nice but his wife is a snob*

GREEN OR BLACK?

To identify class in the countryside have a look at the wellies people are wearing, and what make of car they're driving. The humble but ever-so-practical Wellington boot was made popular by the 1st Duke of Wellington, the victor of Waterloo, in the early 19th century. Nowadays, the aristocracy tends to prefer green ones and drive Range Rovers, while mere mortals wear black ones and drive Mondeos.

Metaphorically Speaking

Metaphor:
They gave us the green light to start the project

Meaning:
They gave us permission to start the project

33

HAVING A LAUGH

It has been said that humour does not travel well, and yet English humour has probably been travelling more successfully for decades than either French brandy or Cuban cigars. The comic genius of Charlie Chaplin, the innuendo of Benny Hill, the absurdity of Monty Python, an ability to poke fun at the establishment and class system in series like *Yes Minister* and *Blackadder,* and a touch of the macabre in *The League of Gentlemen,* are just a few examples of the popular humour England has exported with great success to help keep the world laughing.

When deciding what to pack for a trip abroad there is one thing the English will always take with them; their sense of humour. To the English a person without a sense of humour is like a camel without a hump, and that isn't funny at all, at least not for the camel.

Metaphorically Speaking

Metaphor:
The play had me in stitches

Meaning:
The play was so funny I couldn't stop laughing

RELIGION

It was the Romans who, along with straight roads and central heating, brought Christianity to England. Today, the Anglican Church of England is the official church of England, and is led by the Archbishop of Canterbury who is also the leader of the worldwide Anglican Communion. Canterbury Cathedral became a pilgrimage for Christians around the world after the murder there of Thomas Becket in 1170. Canterbury is such a popular visitor destination you may actually be reading this book while visiting the city right now.

Metaphorically Speaking   *Metaphor:*   *His friends form a broad church*
                                          Meaning: *All sorts of very different people are his friends*

MEETING AND GREETING

The English consider it good manners to shake hands when meeting for the first time, and for formal goodbyes. Handshakes should be firm and dry; trying to crush the bones in the hand you are shaking is a definite faux pas. Do not spend too long holding on to the hand you are shaking – 2-3 seconds is generally enough – and don't forget eye contact; no one trusts anyone who looks down at their shoes while shaking hands.

Although ladies increasingly tend to kiss each other on the cheek when they meet, English men do not hug, and certainly do not kiss anyone other than their wives and close family members, so please keep your distance.

Metaphorically Speaking

Metaphor:
He is a real Sir Walter Raleigh

Meaning:
He is a gentleman (Walter Raleigh laid his coat over a muddy puddle so Queen Elizabeth I would not get her feet dirty. Mind you, it didn't do him much good in the long run; her successor, James I, had him executed)

MANNERS AND FAIR PLAY

It is also an integral part of English social custom to say 'excuse me' if you want to get past someone, 'sorry' if you accidentally bump into someone, 'sorry' if someone bumps into you, 'please' and 'thank you' for absolutely everything, and, of course, to join the back of any and every queue, even if you don't know what you are queuing for.

And finally, we mustn't forget the importance of 'fair play.' The English believe in fair play, and cannot abide cheats. To the English, the game itself and how people behave when playing are far more important than winning or losing. It is far better to lose with grace than win by cheating or simply by trying too hard. The English will almost always support the underdog and a talented amateur is often far more popular than a consummate professional.

Metaphorically Speaking

Metaphor:
We don't seem to be playing on a level playing field

Meaning:
The other person or team has an unfair advantage

BATH AND A CUPPA

Despite the high speed at which many English people live their lives today they still find time to enjoy the important things in life. While the rest of the world takes a shower and drinks coffee, the English prefer to relax in a nice hot bath, and, no matter how hurried life might be, there's always time for a cup of tea.

Metaphorically Speaking   *Metaphor:*   *Mozart isn't really my cup of tea*
                                                 Meaning: *I don't really like Mozart*

MUDDLING THROUGH

Who needs excellence, cares whether things work like clockwork, or go according to plan? Not the English, for, after all, you can always 'muddle through.' The English are great muddlers, in fact, it's a point of national pride. While other nations strive for perfection, the English are happy just to get the job done, somehow, some way. Having muddled through the Spanish Armada, Battle of Trafalgar, Waterloo, a whole Empire, and two world wars, history has surely shown 'muddling through' is the only way to achieve lasting success.

Metaphorically Speaking   *Metaphor: I'm all in a muddle*
                                        Meaning: I am completely confused

FANCY DRESS

If you are approached by anyone dressed in a pinstripe suit, wearing a bowler hat, carrying an umbrella and with a copy of the *Financial Times* under their arm, take a look around; you are probably on *Candid Camera*. England has become a land of relaxed dressers, or even lax dressers. Outside banking, insurance, and some of the more traditional professions, the business suit is being forsaken for more casual modes of dress in the office. Nowadays, baggy jeans, complete with designer bum crack, trainers that cost as much as a Mini did in 1965, and a designer 'T' shirt are the common default dress for many while out doing the weekly shop at ASDA.

Metaphorically Speaking	*Metaphor:*	*He's a bit of a stuffed shirt*
	Meaning:	*He is rather pompous and thinks very highly of himself*

Big Brother and the Police

Big Brother is the government, and if you haven't read George Orwell's *1984* get yourself a copy and make some comparisons. With surveillance cameras everywhere, the English are the most watched people in Europe; someone somewhere must have very square eyes indeed.

Despite all the surveillance, though, the English police is the only national police force in the world to walk the streets unarmed. It doesn't mean England's streets are any safer than elsewhere in the world, but it is nice to be able to ask directions from someone not carrying a sidearm or a machine gun. www.met.police.uk

Metaphorically Speaking

Metaphor: *The police are keeping an eye on him*
Meaning: *The police are watching him*

41

FROM CRADLE TO GRAVE

The NHS was born on 5th July 1948 and has been taking care of the nation's ills ever since. It won't make you pay, and it won't bury you, but it will keep your vaccinations up to date from the day you arrive until the day you depart. It might suffer from a few aches and pains, and even have a touch of arthritis, but it's still probably the best health service in the world, and the English are proud of it, even though it was set up by a Welshman. www.nhs.uk

Metaphorically Speaking   Metaphor: *I am sick of listening to your moaning*
Meaning: *I am very tired of listening to you complaining*

HAVING A CRACKING TIME

The English send more cards annually than any other nation in the world. The first commercial Christmas card in the world was invented by an Englishman, Henry Cole, in 1846. The Christmas cracker is also another firm and established festive favourite in England. A brightly coloured paper tube, containing a paper hat, joke, and small gift, which goes 'pop' when pulled apart, the cracker was invented by Thomas Smith in 1846.

Metaphorically Speaking   Metaphor: *You are absolutely crackers if you don't take an umbrella*
Meaning: *You are very silly if you don't take an umbrella*

NORTH AND SOUTH

Often referred to as the 'north south divide,' there has always been a rivalry between the north of England and the nouth. Exactly where the north begins and the south ends is something that is often open to question. 'Up north' they will tell you that anything below Manchester is south, while 'down south' they often consider anything above the Watford Gap to be 'the north.' Of course, attitudes like this do tend to leave the Midlands in limbo.

For the overseas visitor, however, it is important to know that the stereotypical southerner's image of their northern brethren is of being the slightly thick poor cousins, whereas the stereotype from the north is that southerners are stuck up and pompous. Both sides also think the other has a strange accent. It's all good-humoured rivalry, and always a good topic for a conversation.

Metaphorically Speaking

Metaphor: His parents hit the roof when they found out he wanted to marry a southerner

Meaning: His parents were very angry when they found out he wanted to marry a southerner

LANGUAGE BARRIER

More than steel, coal and motorcars combined, language is probably the most successful 'product' to have ever been exported from England's shores. Between the reigns of Queen Elizabeth I and II the number of mother tongue English speakers in the world has risen from around 7 million in the 16th century to over 400 million in the 21st. Although it is impossible to quote exact figures, conservative estimates today put the number of speakers of English as a second or foreign language at over 500 million, some even as high as a billion.

Unfortunately, the success of English around the world has not helped the English in their attitude to learning a second language, and many of them travel in the expectation that everyone they meet will speak and understand English, often getting very upset and irritated when they don't.

At home, however, the English are extremely tolerant and patient of visitors who struggle to make themselves understood, and will generally do everything they can to do away with the language barrier and ease communication.

Metaphorically Speaking

Metaphor: I am lost for words
Meaning: I don't know what to say

A MINI ROLLS

First introduced in 1959 the Mini is an icon of design and practicality. The one millionth Mini rolled off the production line in March 1965, and by the time production stopped, in 2000, a total of 5,387,862 had been produced. Production of the New Mini started in April 2001 and, on 3rd April 2007, the one millionth New Mini rolled off the Oxford production line. If you want a piece of England get yourself some Mini magic.

At the other end of the scale, of course, we have the ultimate in luxury motoring, the Rolls-Royce. Charles Rolls met Henry Royce in May 1904 at the Midland Hotel in Manchester. They founded Rolls-Royce Limited in 1906 and the motoring legend was born. For years regarded as 'the best car in the world,' the marque is still highly respected and expensive, despite now being owned by our good friends, the Germans. www.rolls-roycemotorcars.com

Metaphorically Speaking

Metaphor: *It is the Rolls-Royce of beers*
Meaning: *It is the best of beers*

LOOK RIGHT BEFORE LEFT

Don't be a hedgehog! Remember, the English sit on the right but drive on the left. But we are not alone! Around one quarter of the world drives on the left. If you are from a country that drives on the left, then good for you; if not, be careful. http://www.dft.gov.uk/pgr/roadsafety/child/

Metaphorically Speaking *Metaphor:* *George is a proper road hog*
Meaning: *George takes up more room on the road than necessary*

RAIL-ROADED

The world's first public railway ran from Stockton to Darlington, and was built by George Stephenson in 1825. Stephenson also built a steam locomotive called 'Rocket.' Though some express trains in England are very fast, and the quickest way around the country, many local ones do not 'rocket' anywhere. If you do decide to let the train take the strain, you will need a rocket scientist to decipher the timetables and fares. www.nationalrail.co.uk

Metaphorically Speaking Metaphor: *You have a one-track mind about food*
Meaning: *All you ever think about is food*

THE TUNNEL

What has the Channel tunnel got to do with being English, you might wonder. Well, to many English people it is an engineering umbilical cord symbolizing the linking of Europe to England. The tunnel officially opened in May 1994. At 31.4 miles (50.5 kilometres), it runs from Folkestone in Kent to Coquelles near Calais, and is the second longest undersea tunnel in the world. If you are in a hurry to leave Paris and get to London you can now cover the 307 miles (495 kilometres) via the tunnel in just 2 hours 15 minutes on the Eurostar. Of course, in your haste, you will miss seeing the wondrous sight of the white cliffs of Dover, but perhaps getting out of France quickly is more important. Vive Le Tunnel!

The white cliffs face continental Europe across the narrowest part of the English Channel, and are historically regarded as a symbolic defence against foreign invasion. Today, however, they shine their welcome to visitors arriving by ferry from the continent. www.whitecliffscountry.org.uk/

Metaphorically Speaking

Metaphor:
He suffers from tunnel vision on that subject

Meaning:
He is very narrow-minded and stubborn on that subject

WEATHER FRONT

Yes, we must mention the weather, everyone else does. It's often cloudy and it can rain quite a lot, but hey, what do you expect, it's England, and we love it. Those that don't, go to Spain, get fed-up with sunshine, and, after a while, return for a bit of good old English rain. www.metoffice.gov.uk

Metaphorically Speaking   *Metaphor:*   *Sorry, but I haven't the foggiest idea*
                                 Meaning: *Sorry but I really don't know*

CRICKET

The most English of games, cricket has been played in England since the mid 1500s, and was spread around the world by English colonists and sailors. The first known 'Laws of cricket' date back to 1744, when the length of the pitch was set at 22 yards. The rules are pretty clear to all who play, so if you don't understand them you obviously come from a country unlucky enough to have escaped our attention in this respect. www.cricinfo.com

Metaphorically Speaking   Metaphor: *This is simply not cricket*
                              Meaning: *This isn't fair*

FOOTBALL

We might not be the best but we were the first; football dates back to 1170 in England. The world's oldest football club playing Association Football to be recognized by both the FA and FIFA is Sheffield Football Club (not to be confused with Sheffield United or Sheffield Wednesday), founded in 1857. Also in Sheffield you will find the world's oldest football ground at Sandygate Road, which first opened in 1804 and is home to Hallam FC. This is also where the world's first inter-club match was played on 26th December 1860 between Hallam FC and Sheffield FC. Despite all this footballing history, however, the English National Football Museum is not to be found in Sheffield, but in Preston in Lancashire. www.football.co.uk

Metaphorically Speaking   *Metaphor:*   *How can you trust them when they keep moving the goal posts?*
Meaning: *How can you trust them when they keep changing the rules?*

BOXING

As the English like to play by the rules it should come as no surprise that the rules of boxing are named after an Englishman; John Sholto Douglas, 9th Marquess of Queensberry, who paid for the publication of the rules drafted by John Chambers in 1867. Prior to this, boxers had followed the 'London Prize Ring Rules' introduced by another Englishman, heavyweight champion Jack Broughton, in 1743.

Metaphorically Speaking   Metaphor: *Hurting his knee was the knockout blow to his chances of winning*
Meaning: *Hurting his knee ended his chances of winning*

THE BOAT RACE

Oxford and Cambridge are, respectively, the oldest and second oldest universities in the English-speaking world, collectively referred to as 'Oxbridge.' The traditional boat race between the universities was first held on 10th June 1829. Cambridge sank in 1859 and 1978, Oxford in 1925 and 1951, and both boats went down in 1912 when the race was started in a virtual gale. At the time of writing the current score stands at 79 to Cambridge, 75 to Oxford, with one controversial dead heat in 1877. It is so popular today that a quarter of a million spectators watch the race from the Thames riverbank every year. www.theboatrace.org

Metaphorically Speaking
    Metaphor: *We are up the creek without a paddle*
    Meaning: *We are in a very difficult situation with no obvious way of getting help*

LONDON

The English are very proud of their capital, for it is from London that democracy, fair play and cricket were brought fourth to an unsuspecting world. In a recorded history dating back over 2000 years, London has survived plague, fire, civil war, aerial bombing, and terrorist attack to grow into one of the most important financial and cultural centres in the world.

The easiest way to get around the city is on the 'Tube,' the world's first underground rail system, which began service between Paddington and Farringdon on the Metropolitan line in 1863. From these modest beginnings the system now has 12 different lines and 204 stations. If you like shopping, hop on either the Bakerloo, Central or Victoria lines to Oxford Circus, and then up to the busiest shopping street in Europe – Oxford Street – a mecca for the ladies (and some gentlemen, too).
www.visitlondon.com

Metaphorically Speaking

Metaphor: *What a capital idea*
Meaning: *What a great idea*

BIRMINGHAM

If music is your thing then there are two cities in England you have to visit. The home town of Ozzy Osbourne, Birmingham is the birthplace of rock legends Black Sabbath, Judas Priest, and Led Zeppelin, which must surely make it the unofficial rock capital of England, possibly Europe, maybe even the world! www.visitbirmingham.com

Metaphorically Speaking

Metaphor:
It was such a whirlwind tour we didn't see very much

Meaning:
We went round so quickly that we didn't see very much

LIVERPOOL

Once your ears have stopped ringing, head north to Liverpool. With 56 number one hits by homegrown artists, the *Guinness Book of Records* recognises Liverpool as being the 'Capital of Pop,' a befitting title for the city that gave the world the Beatles.

The city is also home to the most famous steeplechase in the world, the Grand National, watched by some 600 million people worldwide each year. If you fancy your chances of getting into films, this is also the place to be. After London, Liverpool is the most filmed-in city in England.
www.visitliverpool.com

BLACKPOOL

The biggest and most popular seaside resort in Europe is also home to the £12 million Pepsi Max Big One, Europe's tallest and fastest rollercoaster; ye-ha! If you don't fancy being 'maxed out,' why not join some 3.5 million autumn visitors for what must surely be the most spectacular free public event of its kind anywhere in the world, the Blackpool Illuminations? Dating back to 1879, the illuminations are a dazzling £2.4 million display stretching almost six miles from Starr Gate to Bispham. www.visitblackpool.com

Metaphorically Speaking   *Metaphor:*   *The Pepsi Max Big One is the dog's bollocks*
                                               Meaning: *The Pepsi Max Big One is absolutely fantastic*

STONEHENGE

It's been estimated that Stonehenge took over thirty million man-hours to build, not counting tea breaks. Who says the English don't know how to work hard? Or maybe they were on overtime! www.stonehenge.co.uk

Metaphorically Speaking   *Metaphor:*   *He had been burning the candle at both ends*
                                                Meaning: *He'd been working day and night*

FURTHER INFORMATION

Other websites that might be of interest to visitors:

www.enjoyengland.com

www.english-heritage.org.uk

www.nationaltrust.org.uk

www.pub-explorer.com

www.restaurant-guide.com

What is Morris Dancing? Where can you find the tallest roller coaster in Europe? What do the English really eat for breakfast, and do they really hate the French?

Meet the English is a light-hearted look at some of the history, customs, traditions, people and places that help make England England and the English so very, well, English. If you are English please read on with a light heart and do what the English do best, have a laugh at yourself. If you are a visitor, or are planning to visit England's sometimes sunny, sometimes cloudy and sometimes windy shores, hopefully, this book will help you to at least begin to appreciate – even if not fully understand – the country and its people.

£5.99 UK • $11.95 USA

WWW.VELOCE.CO.UK
WWW.VELOCEBOOKS.COM

ISBN 978-1-845843-62-5

6 36847 04362 9

9 781845 843625

T2-BWV-190